Ten Tips
for Women Who Want to Change the World

Without Losing their Friends, Shirts, or Minds

Paula Prober

T.C.C. Press
Eugene, OR

T.C.C. Press
P.O. Box 50832
Eugene, OR 97405

Printed in the United States of America

ISBN 0-9676842-0-X

Library of Congress Catalog Card Number:
00-190031
Illustrations, format, and cover design by
Kay King
Technical assistance, cover design by K.C. King

Ten Tips
for Women Who Want
to Change the World

Without Losing their
Friends, Shirts,
or Minds

Contents

For in order for our suffering to have any meaning at all, it must ultimately increase the capacity for all humankind both to love and be loved.

Joan Borysenko
Fire in the Soul

to the rainforest women, men, and children

Introduction

This book was written for you if you have felt fear, anger, powerlessness, or despair about the state of the earth. It's for you if curiosity, intensity, guilt, and self-examination have been embedded in your personality since you were two years old. It's for you if you have had to ingest massive amounts of jello or other dangerous substances to get through the day. It's for you if you left your sense of humor at the Mall of America in 1990.

Ten Tips presents very specific strategies for personal development that are designed to provide the push you need to self-actualize, individuate, evolve (pick one), and help humanity get from hate to heart and from greed to grace. The assumption behind the tips is that when we do the challenging work of carefully examining and healing our psyche, we access our authentic, creative, nearly enlightened selves—our goddessness, if you will. With more of our goddessness functioning, we not only create change effectively and compassionately but we also ARE the change. As our small strand in the web of life strengthens, the entire network is transformed. What you have here, then, is a guide to awakening, using, and becoming your higher self. It is my belief that she, your higher self, will know exactly what actions to take to improve life on the planet and that she's the best person for the job.

The tips are based on principles from depth psychology and are influenced by a number of writers, scientists, psychologists, theologians, and artists from Carl Jung to Whoopi Goldberg. I selected the techniques that have been the most helpful to me personally and professionally. Because I suspect that you're leading a busy, probably over-scheduled life, I made *Ten Tips* short and to the point. If you want more information, you will find resources listed at the end of the book that expand on the concepts presented in each tip.

I recommend that you proceed through the tips in order but my greatest concern is that you make this book work for you. Feel free to modify the suggestions or skip some of them altogether. Some of the tips may be more appropriate for you to complete at another time—like, for example, when the kids are grown and you finally have some privacy. Others may involve strategies that feel awkward or uncomfortable to you. Trust yourself. As you work through the tips, be alert for resistance, self-judgment, or fear of criticism from others. This is normal. Feel it. Write about it. And don't let it stop you.

I've focused on women in this book because I know us better, not because I think we're solely responsible for changing the world. I've started studying men and I think that by about 2025, I'll understand them well enough to write their *Ten Tips* book. Not that some of these tips don't apply to men. They do. But I think there's a book for them that would be different in some specific ways. Of course, by 2025, women may have created enough positive change that the *Ten Tips* book for men will be unnecessary. It could happen.

The work of creation was a work of joy whose whole purpose was to bring joy into existence.

...if our inner work is great our outer work will be great, for in it is contained all cosmic dimensions and experiences.

Matthew Fox
The Reinvention of Work

Tip #1
Send Godzilla to Hagerstown

My inner critic's name is Godzilla. She's a body builder whose favorite beverage is Drano. Zilla drives a Mack truck in San Francisco during rush hour for fun and eats hubcaps for breakfast. She has chartreuse eyes, fangs, and hair that would scare your rotweiler. After body building, attacking me is her hobby of choice. As I've grown to know Zilla over the years, her control over me has diminished. We talk, negotiate, and she loosens her grip. I can't get on with changing the world when Godzilla is telling me I'm incompetent and intellectually malfunctioning. Here is a sample of a dialogue I had with Zilla just the other day. Because I've been communicating with her for a while, she's fairly cooperative now. This was not always the case.

Paula: So here we are. We know each other so well, or so it seems. But actually, we both have distorted pictures. You think I'm totally incompetent and I think you are scum.

Godzilla: That's no way to talk to a loyal companion just because I keep track of every time you've ever messed up and remind you of it every day.

P: So, I'm supposed to appreciate you because you never abandon me?

G: Yup.

P: But I WANT YOU to leave.

G: No you don't. I keep you company. What would you do if I were gone?

P: I'd think of something. All right I admit it would be a radical change if you just disappeared, and I don't do all that well with too much change. So, um, do you have any other skills besides slamming me? Could I keep you busy doing something else so you'd lay off the criticism?

G: No. Anyway what would you do with all the time you'd have if you weren't always fighting with me?

P: Take walks, dance around the house, and write books that get published in five languages. What would you do instead of slamming?

G: I told you criticizing is what I do. Listen, maybe I could cut back my hours. Start working part-time. But first you have to acknowledge that I'm not all bad.

P: Well, maybe, but isn't there something else you could do? Take up a hobby? Mud wrestling?

G: No. My purpose in life is to point out your faults and mistakes so you a) won't get too sure of yourself and really mess up, b) won't think you're better than anybody else, c) won't get so successful that people will hate you, and d) don't have to see how messed up your parents were.

15

P: Don't you ever get tired of all this hypervigilance?
G: Yeah. Maybe I could use a vacation. What about that
*   truckers' convention in Hagerstown?*
P: Great idea. I'll e-mail you if I need you.

If you have a critic like Godzilla, consider meeting with her periodically in a journal. Ask her questions about her wants, needs, and purpose. What would help her relax? If you find it embarrassing to talk with a facet of yourself, that's normal. Try using different colored pens for each voice. It will get easier with practice and you may gain new insight or notice an emotional shift. If nothing seems to be happening, try reading the dialogue later. You might be surprised by something you didn't notice at first. For all you visual types, drawing a picture of your critic can improve your rapport with her. If you get to know her well, she might agree to join Zilla in Hagerstown for two weeks. Then you will feel more confident, get more accomplished, and have the energy to tackle Tips 2-10.

The dialogue technique can be used to speak with other aspects of yourself such as your fear, depression, shame, headache, back pain, inner child, wisdom, or creativity. The process is a powerful way to tap into your unconscious. In Jungian psychology, the benefits of working with the unconscious are significant not only to the individual but also to the collective. Over time you can begin to heal wounds from childhood, access your creative problem solving abilities, and explore your spirituality.

Tip #2
Select your committee

Mentors and role models can provide important guidance for women changing the world. Guides are especially valuable when we feel lonely, run out of ideas, or realize we've consumed the entire bag of Oreos in two hours. But good mentors can be hard to find. I mean where do we shop for them? The classifieds? 7-11? And who has the time? My guess is that you recognize the value of this kind of support, may even yearn for it, but end up putting it on the bottom of your list.

Even if you have had mentors in your life from time to time, you may feel, as I do, a need for more diversity or availability. As you concoct your plan for global change, one mentor may, in fact, not be enough. You may require a team of mentors: your very own committee, cheer leading squad, board of directors, or backup singers. One approach is to gather a team that can be on-call 24 hours a day. These are people you respect and admire who do not need to bring their bodies but can just be available in your imagination. I've gathered a fine committee. Each member shares his/her wisdom with me whenever I want it. Here is my team and their most recent suggestions:

Whoopi Goldberg, actress: Keep laughing. This humor is serious business.
Clarissa Pinkola Estes, author: Write every day.
Laura Esquivel, author: Go the creative distance. Take it as far as you can.
Carl Jung, psychotherapist: Don't doubt the quality of your work. Pay attention to your dreams tonight!
Rachel Bagby, musician: Breathe. Sound. Make every sound conscious. From the heart.
Maya Angelou, poet: Have the courage to continue.

Now, if you want your very own mentors, think of people you admire such as authors, artists, scientists, musicians, anthropologists, spiritual leaders, grandparents, or ancestors. List their names. Now pick three or more that you would like to put on your current committee, board, or chorus line. Write about what you imagine each of them could give you. You can create a special notebook to keep track of their wisdom, a kind of *Meetings-with-Mentors* journal. Get a photo or make a symbol of each person to include in the notebook and then schedule appointments when you need them. Ask for advice. Picture them drinking tea or walking beside you or singing in a kick line behind you.

If you have difficulty imagining people, mentors can come in other forms. Do you have a favorite animal who can serve as a teacher? Do you have experiences with any spiritual guides? Perhaps you have a spiritual practice where you access an inner source of wisdom or you feel a deep connection with nature. Any of these will serve nicely as mentors.

If you have had experiences in childhood that continue to be painful, try taking one of your mentors with you back to a specific event. Rewrite the event as if your mentor were there and had changed the outcome. Notice how you feel as you write. Then take time to feel the different outcome in your mind and body. If you feel overwhelmed by wounds from childhood, a committee can help but will probably not be enough. Consider seeking out a good therapist, one who is sensitive, bright, and has experience as a client. Many people are reluctant to begin a counseling process for a variety of reasons. Sit quietly with one of your mentors and explore the pros and cons of psychotherapy.

The person who commits him[her]self to a life of continuing confrontation with the unconscious within him[her]self, will also confront the unknown in the world at large with an open mind, and what is more, with a heart of wisdom... unless consciousness changes, the world cannot change.

June Singer
Boundaries of the Soul

Tip #3
Seek out your self-doubt

Let me introduce you to Sadie, my self-doubt. She resembles my Hungarian ancestors so you may notice her accent. It's OK with me if you laugh at her. She is purposely exaggerated. I'll explain why after you've met her.

So, you vish to get to know me better? First, I suppose I'm persistent. That's my most memorable trait. Vell, besides the fact that I ask a lot of ridiculous and irrelevant questions. I just vant to understand the situation thoroughly and know all of the implications from every angle all the time. Is that asking too much? I just don't vant to miss anything or misunderstand anything or make a mistake. I hate being any kind of incorrect. Politically, socially, morally, intellectually, spiritually, biologically, mathematically, gastronomically, astrologically. You never knew there vere all these vays to be incorrect, did you?

Anyvay, I'm depressed because I vould like to look like the models. You know, the ones who look so smooth, so neat, so undisturbed. But is impossible. The stripes go van vay and the buttons the other. And, you see, I have this fat hair. The hair on my head is never quite sure of vhere to go or vhat to do. It is constantly out of control and not in a small subtle vay that is easy to hide. It is out of control in a big vay. It is embarrassing also because these hairs drop out indiscriminately anyvhere at anytime. People think I'm leaving them souvenirs or something but this is not how I vant to be remembered. It is so depressing because even if I am perfect in every other vay, there is my fat hair spoiling everything.

But I'm not perfect in every other vay. And I find that to be a major problem. Certainly I'm not asking to be extremely perfect. I know my limits. I just think slightly perfect vould be nice.

You might think I'd advise you to strangle your self-doubt or just say buzz off to her. But, no, she's another part of yourself you should know intimately. When she goes underground, she just gets more obnoxious. It's normal to have self-doubt. Bright women, who, by the way, we (you and me) are, often have more self-doubt than most because of our tendency to be analytical. In our thirst for knowledge, self-awareness, and higher levels of moral development, we question, oh, everything— our motives, our ethics, our sanity, and our questioning. Giving a voice to my self-doubt has helped me understand her and laugh at how dedicated she is. If I'm going to have her in my home, which is inevitable, I may as well make her comfortable. Then she won't keep me from taking the risks I need to take in order to change the world.

To hear from your own self-doubt, write a monologue. Reflect on self-doubt's nature. What are her insecurities? What does she worry about? When does she get way out of line? Give her a name. Have her describe herself in great detail. Let her go on a tirade. Have her babble, complain, or whisper and tell her story. Include anything that helps you see her more clearly; include hobbies, career, quirks, dress, purpose, interests, physical traits, loves/hates. Avoid being polite. Exaggerate. When you make her larger than life, you'll find that she shrinks.

As you write your monologue, see if you feel some relief; you may even want to laugh. If you need a more physical connection, try reading the speech aloud using appropriate body language, dramatic flair, clothing, and hair style. If you notice her throwing a tantrum in the future, take a moment to let her vent. This will give you more clarity around what is blocking your ability to move forward.

You can use monologues for many aspects of yourself. Once I wrote one for despair. I was shocked to discover someone loving who wanted to hold me in her arms and rock me. I have seen despair differently ever since.

Tip #4
Get your "inner bitch" to exercise her rights

———

Browsing through my favorite bookstore one day, I came across *Getting in Touch with Your Inner Bitch*, by Elizabeth Hilts. It's a short, funny book that makes an important point. Women who learn how to be assertive and how to let go of their "toxic niceness" are happier, healthier, and better prepared to change the world. This bitch is not mean or abusive. She simply knows how to set limits and be powerful; her compassion stays completely intact. Hilts suggests that we practice using the phrase "I don't think so" when tempted to agree to do something for someone else that that person can do perfectly well for him or herself. Often, instead of saying "no," we give up our own ideas, our time, our independence, and perhaps even our souls. Sometimes, fears around setting limits and saying "no" begin in childhood. One way to explore the fear is to write a letter, that you don't send, to a friend or partner with whom this is an issue. Because you aren't sending the letter, you don't have to censor anything and empathy is unnecessary. Here's part of a sample letter I wrote to a friend:

> *I am so sick of your neediness and martyrdom. You sit there and just expect me to save you, to call, to apologize, to be available always. You expect me to drop everything for you. You don't listen. You turn the conversation back to yourself or glance around checking to see if anyone is admiring you. It's disgusting. I'm tired of it. You're stuck in a narcissistic stage that you'll never escape. . .*

As I reread this, I looked to see if it reminded me of anyone from my past. Who else needed to hear this? Sure enough, the traits described here were a combination of characteristics belonging to my parents. In releasing the anger in the letter, I found a deeper issue that needed attention. Then I could put my relationship with my friend in perspective. The next step was to decide how I really felt about the friend and have my inner bitch help me communicate tactfully, using honesty, self-control, and compassion.

Now write your own unsent, uncensored letter. See if in releasing the intense feelings, you gain more courage to say "no" when you mean "no."

You may feel some resistance to finding the bitch. See if you have any of the following thoughts and put a check mark next to them:

- I can't stand conflict. I keep the peace at all costs.
- It's important to be nice.
- I'll be left alone if I express my true self.
- What will the neighbors think?
- I've always done it this way. So have my mother, aunt, grandmother, sister, and cousin.
- My ideas are stupid.
- I want to be liked.
- I don't know what I really think.
- I have better control when I go along.
- When I'm busy, I don't have to feel.

Notice the sentences you checked. This will help you see more reasons why assertiveness is difficult. Now try the next suggestion.

Make a list of everything you do in a week (or a day if you have major workaholic tendencies). Categorize the list into Must-Do, Choose-to-Do, Stop-Do-

ing. Prioritize the Stop-Doing list. Then go to the gym with the bitch and ask her to help you build up your "I-don't-think-so" muscles. Next, begin with item number one on the Stop list. As you say "no" to each activity, notice how the sky does not fall on your head.

Repeat the following mantra: The planet needs me to stop wasting time taking care of the wrong things.

Tip #5
Make more noise

I have always been sensitive to sound and moved by music. I cry when groups of people are singing anything, anytime, anywhere. My cousin Sue says I've had this annoying habit of humming unconsciously since I was three. Often, when receiving a massage, I make odd noises to release emotion or move the energy. Sounds are a big part of my life.

As I became more aware of this about eight years ago, I started using sound for myself therapeutically. One of the forms this took was a process called sounding or toning. The toning that I do—there are many different kinds—starts off quite simply. I sit for ten to twenty minutes and spontaneously make sounds: hums, whooshes, notes, tunes, creaks, moans, sighs, squeaks. Whatever sounds needing expression are allowed out.

I know it can be uncomfortable and frightening to let sounds out, even the prettier ones. You may have been told that speaking, singing, sighing, gasping, groaning, grunting, growling, sobbing, screaming, and screeching were not appropriate activities for young ladies. How silly. You need your voice, all of it, if you're going to change the world. With toning, you are gaining courage and giving yourself permission to be heard while also getting the added benefit of releasing tension and emotion.

Now, for those of you who have partners, kids, and pets, you might have trouble finding a time and location where you can do this and avoid almost certain humiliation. Try toning in your car when you are alone as a way to begin. You can also sing, chant, or OM, for starters. As you gain confidence, select a safe place in your home or outdoors to sit comfortably and tone. I have found toning to be much like meditation. Doing it regularly, over time, it becomes possible to get in touch with a deep feeling of peace fairly quickly. Toning might be a good alternative if you have had difficulty with traditional meditation. Expect connections to your spirituality and the larger universe. If you can find others willing to risk embarrassment, tone in a group. The synergy can be magical.

If you are more visual than auditory, you may be more comfortable at first making noise with paints, pencils, crayons, or pastels. Then examine your drawing and see if it has something to say, sing, or shout. If you have dancing tendencies, you might need to move while toning; consider spontaneously choreographing your sounding.

The effect of each person's individual commitment resounds throughout the universe, creating resonant pathways, sounding reverberant notes, restoring the web of connection in a great song of healing.

Caitlin Matthews
Singing the Soul Back Home

Tip #6
Enlighten up

———————

It's taken me years to develop a sense of humor. My friends tell me I've evolved from serious and reserved to occasionally witty and mildly entertaining. And yet, people still tell me to lighten up. I want to punch them. "How can I possibly lighten up when there is so much to worry about," I say. But I understand their good, although misguided, intentions. I prefer to *en*lighten up, which is a process that allows me to be both intense and funny at the same time. It involves prayer, candles, goddesses, and my greatest fear. Here's what I do.

I design a special candle to honor the goddess of my greatest fear and I pray to her in those moments when I'm overwhelmed with anxiety and rumination. Often, this takes the form of bagladyphobia. I get flooded with images of me in my earmuffs and overcoat wandering around downtown Chicago babbling about how Ronald McDonald is my hero. It isn't pretty.

The prayer is typed and glued to a glass jar that contains a votive candle and reads as follows:

To Paula's Controlling Goddess of the Eternal Bag
I honor your bag womaness and ask that you collect all of
my anxieties, including:
- *fears of poverty, chastity, and obedience*
- *ghastly images of mental and physical incapacitation*
- *anal-retentive tendencies to obsess about my compulsive need for angst*
- *desire to control such things as: guests in my house moving objects that are always supposed to stay where they are, other people's opinions of me, the building of any nuclear power plants anywhere in the world, my hair curling.*

Please place the above items in your shopping cart and bless them for their portability. Amen.

If you wish to create your own enlightening since laughter and light are necessary for world changing, here's what you can do:

1. Think of your greatest fear or, if that's too scary right now, think of a part of yourself that you find particularly annoying.

2. Write a prayer to the goddess of your fear or annoying trait.

3. Find a glass container and votive candle that you like.

4. Look for a magazine or greeting card image that fits or draw your own.

5. Type up your description so it will fit on the container. Glue it on. For a longer lasting model, cover the paper with a product called Mod Podge (available at craft stores).

6. Light your candle when you need reassurance or a good laugh.

You can also use a candle to honor a part of your psyche that needs more attention and respect like your courage, inner child, or your commitment to a better world. The act of candle lighting can be a quick way to remind yourself of what's important on those days when you feel hopeless or overwhelmed.

Tip #7
Do lunch with your evil twin

———————

As you may have gathered by now, I believe that if you want to change the world, you must deal with your demons. Carl Jung said, "We do not reach enlightenment by imagining figures of light but by making the darkness conscious. The latter procedure, however, is disagreeable, and therefore not popular." So take the trip into your psychic basement and grab your evil twin. In Jungian terms, the twin is the shadow, the part or parts of ourselves that: we reject, deny, hide, and hate. If we don't deal with these parts, we risk projecting them onto others. This can wreck relationships at best and create evil empires at worst. And don't tell me you don't do shadow work because that's negative thinking and you have a big bag of positive thoughts and that's all you need. Right. Put those affirmations up against your evil twin. Guess who wins.

Hey, I know this is tough stuff. And large numbers of people try to avoid it by thinking they can and should just move on and, well, they don't even have basements. Uh huh. I don't see that philosophy working. Not in any deeply significant, long-term sort of way. I get irritated just thinking about it. If you could see me now, you'd notice the tension increasing in the back of my neck. This stresses me out because I see so many people's evil twins running amok. It's a skill I have. These people often think they are making great sacrifices for humanity. Then I go a little crazy. I know you've known some of them. I know I don't want to be one.

Let me introduce you to Paulette, my evil twin. I found Paulette one day when a relationship I thought was THE relationship ended. I was a mess and my usual coping strategies were not working. I got out my journal and let the worst of me speak. Here's a portion of what she said:

I'm Paulette, Paula's evil twin. I embody everything mean, creepy, and scary about Paula. Needless to say, she's not too fond of me, but I don't really care. I'm constantly angry and I hate everything and everyone. Paula finds that difficult to accept but I just tell her, "Hey look. It's who I am. Take it or leave it." She, of course, would like to leave it, but I won't let her do that.

Oh. Did I say that I'm totally obsessed all of the time about something? Well, recently I have been obsessed about sex. I'm constantly searching for the partner who can meet my every need. And I have many needs. Sex is just one. But then I haven't done it in so long, hell, I don't know if I really remember what to do. But I'm willing to give it a try if I could just get a hold of someone. Anyway, I know that it's been so long since Paula's been laid because she just doesn't have what it takes to attract a partner. I tried writing a few personal ads for her. She didn't get any response. I don't know why. They were damn good. Like: "DF, 47, tired of rejection. You tell me I'm beautiful or I break your arm." Now don't you think that shoulda worked? Oh my. I could go on and on about Paula. After all, I know her about as good as anybody. Sometimes she acts like a nice girl to prove she's lovable or she is Madam Super Achiever to hide her fear that she's really stupid. How sick is that? Then she pretends that I don't exist but you can be sure I don't stand for that. I WILL NOT BE IGNORED. She'll pay if she tries to do her life without me. I have ways of making her and anyone within 30 feet of her totally miserable for extended periods of time.

And you can't blame me. I'm from a family of obsessive control freaks. It's in my bloodline. And there ain't no transfusions that'll cure this genetic defect. After all, we're talking generations here. Ancestry. If you expect little old me to break the mold, y'all been watching too much PBS or hanging around too much electromagnetic radiation.

Isn't she something? After writing that, I felt relieved and didn't have to act out my anger, loss, and loneliness on some innocent bystander. I found that even the worst of me was not so terrible. Looking Paulette in the face was preferable to hiding her in the snake pit behind my house where she could get really ugly. And just in case you were wondering, the evil twin is not evil. In fact, she holds some of your best stuff. I'm asking you to do lunch with her so that you can discover it's safe to take her out in public. She may even have some qualities you need and admire. What are the positive traits that you hide or reject? Creativity? Intellect? Passion? As you acknowledge your shadow, these parts become accessible, making global consciousness-raising easier.

I should warn you though. This tip should only be attempted if you've been in therapy several years or you come from a healthy family. Seriously, my self-esteem was quite fragile for some time and even the label "evil twin" would have made me cringe. It wasn't funny then. The way to decide when you're ready is if you can handle the thought that your shadow may remind you of your parents and you can imagine laughing at how totally terrible she is.

So, if you are ready, here are the steps:
1. Think of people you know who have traits that you can't stand. This can include "positive" characteristics that annoy you. (Jung talks a lot about how we project our shadow onto others.)
2. List the traits.
3. Think about how you are when you are at your worst. List those traits.

4. Create a character from those lists. Include whatever details help bring her into clearer focus: lifestyle, physical appearance, obsessions, passions, bad habits, favorite expressions, number of divorces, criminal record, hobbies, sick thoughts. Write all this as a monologue in her voice.

5. Exaggerate.

If it's not the time to meet your own evil twin, here's another possibility. Imagine that there's a dark knight of the soul ready to meet with you and share important information. Picture him in your mind having power, wisdom, and embodying some of your repressed life force. Schedule a time and place to meet him and listen to what he has to say. See him as an ally. When it's time, he can introduce you to your evil twin.

The woman who takes the time to grow herself in the darkness becomes familiar—perhaps for the first time—with the real source and containment of her psychic strength...And what is the real thing, the thing for which she longs? The love affair with her own spirit, the inner marriage that commits her to her destiny, the rituals of soul that feed her deepest hunger, and the sense of being pregnant with her Self, her creative essence.

Jill Mellick
Coming Home to Myself

Tip #8
Make more love

How's your love life? Remember when people asked you that? I've been single for years and dateless for many of them so I would often end up saying "Lousy" or "Nonexistent." But the truth is, there's a ton of love in my life. It comes from many sources: friends, family, music, books, trees, toning, spiritual guides, gentle breezes, gorgeous sunsets, and myself, on my better days. It has taken years of therapies, reading, spiritual practice, journal writing, obsessing, and kvetching to get here— that is, to accept love from others without thinking that I don't deserve it, and to finally understand that there's a big Love that is accessible always and, by the way, doesn't leave socks on the floor..

The task here is to find ways to bring love into your life and then to find ways to give it away. Changing the world requires great gobs of love.

To begin, make a list of where, when, and how you feel love. Remember to include those precious moments when you see the first green leaves of spring, when you feel the sun on your back after a week of gray skies, when a spiritual experience lands in your lap, or when someone else takes the kids to basketball practice. Use colors, drawings, diagrams, or collage to make them vivid.

Perhaps you are single right now, feeling lonely, and grieving over the loss of a partner. Write the letter you wish you had received from the person who left you. Here's a portion of one I wrote three years ago:

Dear Paula,

I should have loved you more. You deserved it. I know I'm a fool but I was scared. Eventually you would have realized that I'm no match for you. Then what? Either you would've left me or your soul would've been weeping if you had tried to dismantle yourself to make the relationship work. You are an elegant woman and one who deserves an equally brilliant partner. . .

You get the idea.

Or, write a love letter to yourself from someone real or imagined who clearly knows how totally lovable you are. Consider developing an ongoing journal relationship with this someone. If you feel close to nature, sit outdoors and ask for help from the spirits of the ocean, the woods, or your backyard. One way to do this that's particularly Jungian is to write from the point of view of your ideal inner partner. What is this part of you like? How does this part love you? Bringing this aspect to consciousness provides access to the traits in yourself that that you are looking for in the Other.

You also might want to experiment with some hands-on love. Wait, no, this is not about masturbation. I'm talking sensuous, not sexual, here. Take a few minutes in the morning before you get out of bed or in the evening before falling asleep, or in the shower, to consciously stroke your skin and mentally send love to yourself through your hands. You may be surprised at how much pleasure you feel. When I've done this, it feels as if I'm creating new brain pathways, connections that didn't get made in infancy. I started this practice when I got tired of waiting for someone else to do it.

And now, even if there were someone else, I'd continue.
Try it. Use some lotion or massage oil if you have more
time. Some days I just rub my feet, amazed at how well
they hold me up and hardly ever complain.

If you are quite uncomfortable with these suggestions, you might be coming up against some old entrenched critical messages. It may mean that you need to try some of the therapies and kvetching I referred to earlier. If you've had a childhood that was at all difficult, you are likely to be carrying some extra luggage that will get in the way at the wrong times. It will get heavy and pile up around you so you can't get to the phone. A good therapist can help you sort out what belongs to you and what you can return to family members. Your load can be lightened considerably. Without all those bags, you will have the energy, awareness, and receptivity to catch the Love yourself and then toss it back out into the world. I know about this because I was the luggage queen. I could hardly move around my house. There were bags all over the place. Love was squished under the stacks of Samsonite. But that's changed. And the planet breathes more easily.

We are being directed in the evolutionary process by divine guides through our dreams, our symptoms, our planet. New values are emerging—feminine values and masculine values that are free of patriarchal abuse. A totally new harmonic lies ahead in the new millennium.

Marion Woodman
Coming Home to Myself

Tip #9
Appreciate your nerdliness

I apologize for calling you nerdly. You may not be. But in my mind, nerdliness is a good thing and I will be the first one to stand up and admit my own nerdly status. You realize, of course, that this means we are very smart, sensitive, intuitive, intense, and creative. These are not bad traits. These characteristics just may not make us popular. And so we are labeled nerd-like, nerdsome, or nerdescent.

Women who obsess about making a difference on the planet which, admit it, you do, are probably brighter than average and may be even, shall I say it, intellectually, creatively, and/or intuitively gifted. If you don't believe me, take this handy test I've devised. Answer the following questions:

1. Are you able to experience complex emotions, analyze the effect of America's conspicuous consumption on poverty in Bangladesh, read Tolstoy, and cook spaghetti all at the same time?

2. Do people tell you to lighten up when you are just trying to enlighten them?

3. Does your intuition work overtime so you know how family members, neighbors and stray dogs feel even before they do?

4. Do you worry about everything and then worry about your worrying?

5. Do you have so many ideas and interests that you are in a constant state of precocious perfectionist paralysis?

6. Do you wonder how you can feel like not enough and too much at the same time?

7. Do you get stuck for days in moral dilemmas that your peers don't even recognize as dilemmas?

8. Are you embarrassed to tell people that it's

easier for you to fall in love with ideas than with humans?

9. Do you see ecru, beige, sand, and eggshell when others see white?

10. Do you question how you will ever contribute to healing the planet when you find yourself frequently imagining twelve ways to wrap your neighbor's leaf blower around her head?

If you answered 'yes' to at least five, you qualify. But if you're still not convinced I'm not surprised. Gifted women often see their abilities as the result of hard work or luck. Yet, in understanding this, you can begin to see that traits like intensity, hypersensitivity, introspection, intuition, and perfectionism may not be neuroses (as you've secretly suspected) but may be giftedness. This is an important distinction. It can help you to be more self-accepting. Then your intellect and creativity work for you, and for others, which is what this book is all about. Right?

If you worry that this means you are developing

a superior attitude, relax. Humans can be equal and different at the same time. Everyone has gifts to contribute. You have a right to acknowledge yours. And you will be a more effective change-maker if you do. A metaphor might help.

You are a rainforest: complex, resourceful, fragile, intense, lively, multidimensional.
Your friend, Harriet, is a desert and your neighbor Beth

is a meadow. Each ecosystem has beauty and value; they're just different.

Often, women with rainforest traits are both highly sensitive and analytical. There is usually a deep need for balance, beauty, and justice. You may rejoice in the almost perfect piano sonata or experience pleasure in the precise moment when the balance between light and darkness changes the color of the leaves on the vine maples in your yard. Others may misunderstand your sensitivities and see you as judgmental, impatient, inefficient, and obsessive. And, in fact, you may have difficulty not criticizing others who don't "get it." Yet, you also judge your own behavior relentlessly. One way to examine this more is to spend 15 minutes writing about this type of intrinsic perfectionism, which is what I call it. Use a stream of consciousness approach. See if you can let the thoughts flow, and if you can't, write about that.

When the search for precision and harmony is thwarted and misinterpreted and the analysis is turned inward, fear of failure may be one result. As usual, I can relate. I've avoided activities that might result in embarrassment or, heaven forbid, shall I say it, a mistake.

What helps is to make a list of activities that you would like to do that you avoid for fear of doing them imperfectly. Choose two, write them on your calendar, and then do them! This is especially important if you have children, so you show them that mistakes are OK. Write about your experiences afterward. How did you survive? What self-talk did you use to get yourself through?

Understanding the complexity and beauty of your nerdescence can release blocked capacities and open up new horizons. When you give yourself permission to see what you see, to feel what you feel, and to know what you know, the world of possibilities expands not just for you but for the collective.

In *Little Women,* Jo's mother says to her, "You have so many extraordinary gifts. How can you expect to live an ordinary life?" Sit with this statement. What do you notice? Imagine that your mother said this to you. Write or draw your thoughts, feelings, and reactions.

Tip #10
Consider the altar-natives

———————

Changing humankind requires divergent thinking—the ability to go beyond the conventional to the imaginative, the mysterious, the unusual, and the unexpected. This is not particularly easy since it can mean holding contradiction in one hand and ambiguity in the other. Many of the tips have asked you to venture into these creative realms. These last suggestions are designed to stir up your psyche once more and integrate the experiences from tips 1-9.

Find a spot to sit quietly. Use whatever tools you already have to help yourself relax into a slightly altered state. Breathe. Now get a visual image of the hopelessness or fear you have felt about world events. What do you see? Colors? Objects? Symbols? Sit with the image until you feel that it is a true representation of this feeling. Draw it, or paint it, or describe it in words. Give it a title. Then use the same process to get a visual image of the ideal world— the way you wish things could be or the goal you are working toward. Draw it, or paint it, or describe it, and title it. Then, in a process that could take days or weeks, make a series of drawings of the steps from image one to image two. Let this process be intuitive and the drawings symbolic. Notice how you feel as you draw. These images can allow you to shift perceptions and to find solutions that were previously unavailable.

Next, find a place in your home to build a small altar. Collect sacred objects, photos, stones, candles, and drawings. Decide what you need to honor in your life at this time: your child self, relationships, community, diversity, courage, Earth, connection to nature and spirit, fear, inner bitch, evil twin, tolerance, humor, time, art, safety, orgasms. Design your altar accordingly and acknowledge this part of you regularly. Change the items on the altar occasionally. An altar can be a visual

reminder of who you really are and why you are here.
When you wonder if it's all worth it, let your altar say,
"Yes, most definitely, uh huh."

And finally, design a ritual to evaluate and commemorate your work with the tips. Select a time when you will not be disturbed. You can make it simple— a quiet moment with a cup of tea reflecting on your process and congratulating yourself. Or you can make it elaborate—invite your newly identified selves and your committee members to a party. Light your enlighten up candle and put on some dancing music. You might imagine yourself dancing with a partner. Feel yourself loving and being loved. Use all of your senses. Allow this partner and you to expand and fill the space and, then, grow beyond the room so that the energy of this love touches all the beings of the world who aren't dancing. Let feelings of gratitude pulse through you— appreciation for your courage, and thankfulness for the circumstances that have brought you to this time and this place.

Conclusion

Congratulations! If you have put all ten tips into action, you can now become a member of WRGTPSHFEH— Women Reaching Goddessness Through Psychology, Spirituality, and Humor in order to Facilitate the Evolution of Humanity. You can call it WRFEH (pronounced 'ruff') for short. When changing the world, colleagues are important. As a member of WRFEH, you get a place to visit where you can be reassured that you're not alone and you're not going crazy. For now, I will give you places to reach me. My e-mail address is pprober@efn.org, snail mail is P.O. Box 50832, Eugene, OR 97405, web page is www.psychevolution.com. Eventually, I'll want you to reach other members of WRFEH so your inner critics can plan vacations together in exotic environments.

In the meantime, remember that smart, complicated women can grasp concepts intellectually in five minutes or less while emotional healing takes much longer. Give yourself plenty of time to change and permission to move slowly. You may feel a sense of urgency as you think about world events. I know I do. But I also keep in mind that every small step makes a difference and that our concept of time is limited by a physical reality that may exist only in our imaginations.

As you start to change, you may notice that you resist your own evolution. It can be frightening to let go of old patterns, behaviors, and beliefs. It's unfamiliar territory being your authentic, creative, nearly enlightened self. Perhaps you won't recognize her after she shows up and then when you do you may not be sure you want her. She might embarrass you in public or decide you are too weird. Consider the possibility that you are rediscovering the real you— the you who naturally feels joy and love, compassion and connection to what June Singer calls "the fabric of the universe." And that it may take time to adjust to the whole fabric after thinking you were just hanging by a thread.

And if you're looking for proof that the world is a better place, I suggest you look for evidence in the everyday things. Are you more assertive in relationships? Are you coming up with new ways to solve old problems? Do you have more energy? Are you more loving and relaxed with your children? Do you laugh more often? Are family members more cooperative? Is your To-Do list shorter? Are you making time to nourish yourself and not feeling guilty? Are you aware of feeling less fearful and less angry? Are the people in your life emotionally healthier? Are you finding concrete ways to be of service in your community that have less to do with ego and more to do with love? When you agree to get involved in an activist organization, are you energized rather than resentful? Are you doing work that you love? Do you wonder why you are on planet Earth but trust that there is a good reason and that you will find it? Do you have moments in nature or in a creative process when you know there is more to reality than what we call reality? Are you open to communication from the invisible world? Are you open to giving and receiving love in new ways? Are you experiencing moments of pure joy and gratitude?

Those are clues that change is occurring. You might think that it's still all very personal, but the threads that make the fabric are woven together. Your growth can not help but affect the entire system so that you make a difference, personally and globally. If we are, in fact, interconnected in that incredibly complex web of life, then, as each of us journeys toward greater consciousness, the entire system changes. Your commitment to deep inner development transforms the world. The path from hate to heart and from greed to grace may be only ten tips away.

Resources for More Information

Introduction

Institute of Noetic Sciences, 475 Gate Five Road, Suite 300, Sausalito, CA 94965; (415) 331-5653; www.noetic.org

Roszak, T., Gomes, M.E., Kanner, A.D. (1995). *Ecopsychology: Restoring the earth, healing the mind.* San Francisco: Sierra Club.

Singer, J. (1990). *Seeing through the visible world: Jung, gnosis, and chaos.* San Francisco: Harper & Row.

Tart, C. T. (1986). *Waking up: Overcoming the obstacles to human potential.* Boston: Shambhala.

Walker, A. (1992). *Possessing the secret of joy.* New York: Harcourt Brace.

Tip 1: Send Godzilla to Hagerstown

Baldwin, C. (1990). *Life's companion: Journal writing as a spiritual quest.* New York: Bantam.

Cameron, J. (1996). *The vein of gold: A journey to your creative heart.* New York: Tarcher.

Metzger, D. (1992). *Writing for your life: A guide and companion to the inner worlds.* San Francisco: Harper.

Ferrucci, P. (1982). *What we may be: Techniques for psychological and spiritual growth through psychosynthesis.* New York: Tarcher.

Tip 2: Select your committee

Angelou, M. (1981). *The heart of a woman.* New York: Random House.

Arnold, K.D., Noble, K. D. Subotnik, R. F. (1996). *Remarkable women: Perspectives on female talent development.* Cresskill NJ: Hampton.

Cowan, T. (1996). *Shamanism as a spiritual practice for daily life.* Freedom CA: Crossing Press.

Matthews, C. (1995). *Singing the soul back home.* Rockport MA: Element.

Tip 3: Seek out your self-doubt

Aron, E. N. (1996) *The highly sensitive person: How to thrive when the world overwhelms you.* Secaucus NJ: Carol.

Glendinning, C. (1994). *My name is Chellis and I'm in recovery from Western civilization.* Boston: Shambhala.

Singer, J. (1994). *Boundaries of the soul: The practice of Jung's psychology.* New York: Doubleday.

Tip 4: Get your inner bitch to exercise her rights

Hilts, E. (1994). *Getting in touch with your inner bitch.* Bridgeport CT: Hysteria.

Houston, J. (1982). *The possible human: A course in extending your physical, mental, and creative abilities.* Boston: Tarcher.

Noble, K. (1994). *The sound of a silver horn: Reclaiming the heroism in contemporary women's lives.* New York: Columbine.

Tip 5: Make more noise

Dewhurst-Maddock, O. (1993). *The book of sound therapy: Heal yourself with music and voice.* New York: Simon & Schuster.

Gardner, K. (1990). *Sounding the inner landscape.* Stonington, ME: Caduceus.

Hale, S. E. (1995). *Song and silence: Voicing the soul.* Albuquerque NM: La Alameda.

Keyes, L. E. (1973). *Toning: The creative power of the voice.* Marina del Rey CA: DeVorss.

Tip 6: Enlighten up

Baldwin, C. (1990). *Life's companion: Journal writing as a spiritual quest.* New York: Bantam.

Fox, M. (1991). *Creation spirituality: Liberating gifts for the peoples of the earth.* San Francisco: Harper.

Macy, J. (1991). *World as lover, world as self.* Berkeley CA: Paralax.

Tip 7: Do lunch with your evil twin

Abrams, J. ed. (1994). *The shadow in America: Reclaiming the soul of a nation.* Novato CA: Nataraj.

Johnson, R. A. (1986). *Inner work: Using dreams and active imagination for personal growth.* San Francisco: Harper & Row.

Johnson, R. A. (1991). *Owning your own shadow: Understanding the dark side of the psyche.* San Francisco: Harper.

Zweig, C., Abrams, J. eds. (1991). *Meeting the shadow: The hidden power of the dark side of human nature.* Los Angeles: Tarcher.

Tip 8: Make more love

Berry, T. (1988). *The dream of the earth.* San Francisco: Sierra Club.

Esquivel, L. (1996). *The law of love.* New York: Crown.

Houston, J. (1987). *The search for the beloved: Journeys in sacred psychology.* Los Angeles: Tarcher.

Roszak, T. (1992). *The voice of the earth: An exploration of ecopsychology.* New York: Touchstone.

Sheldrake, R. (1991). *The rebirth of nature: The greening of science and God.* New York: Bantam.

Tip 9: Appreciate your nerdliness

Clark, B. (1997) *Growing up gifted.* Upper Saddle River NJ: Prentice-Hall.

Institute for the study of advanced development. 1452 Marion St., Denver, CO 80218. (303) 837-8378; www.gifteddevelopment.com

Kerr, B. A. (1994). *Smart girls: A new psychology of girls, women, and giftedness.* Scottsdale AZ: Gifted Psychology.

Miller, A. (1981). *The drama of the gifted child.* New York: Basic.

Silverman, L. K. (1993). *Counseling the gifted and talented.* Denver, CO: Love.

Tip 10: Consider the altar-natives

Borysenko, J. (1993). *Fire in the soul: A new psychology of spiritual optimism.* New York: Warner.

Fox, M. (1994). *The reinvention of work: A new vision of livelihood for our time.* San Francisco:Harper.

Estes, C. P. (1992). *Women who run with the wolves.* New York: Ballantine.

Kingsolver, B. (1995). *High tide in Tucson.* New York: HarperCollins

Macy, J. (1998). *Coming back to life: Practices to reconnect ourlives, our world.* BC Canada: New Society.

Osbon, D.K. (1991). *Reflections on the art of living: A Joseph Campbell companion.* New York: HarperCollins.

Utne Reader—The Best of the Alternative Media. P.O. Box 7459, Red Oak, IA 51591-2459; www.utne.com.

Woodman, M., Mellick, J. (1998). *Coming home to myself: Reflections for nurturing a woman's body & soul.* Berkeley:Conari.

The privilege of a lifetime is being who you are.

We must be willing to get rid of the life we've planned, so as to have the life that is waiting for us.

The goal of the hero trip down to the jewel point is to find those levels in the psyche that open, open, open, and finally open to the mystery of your Self being the Buddha consciousness or the Christ. That's the journey.

Joseph Campbell
A Joseph Campell Companion

About the Author

Paula Prober, M.S., M.Ed. is a licensed professional counselor in private practice in Eugene, Oregon. She has writen articles on precocious children for the Eugene *Register-Guard* and on gifted adults for the journal *Advanced Development.* She writes a regular column in University of Oregon's TAGLine, a newsletter for parents of exceptionally bright youngsters that is distributed throughout the state and she facilitates classes for these parents and for gifted women. When not counseling, writing, or facilitating, you can find Ms. Prober doing the Argentine tango.

About the Illustrator

Kay King is an artist and a teacher in Eugene, Oregon. She earned her fine arts degree from Seton Hall College in Pennsylvania and her teaching degree from the University of Oregon. She has taught gifted children for nearly twenty years. This is her second book.

Acknowledgments

You might think that with a book this size there wouldn't be many people to thank. But there are. Hordes of them, actually, if you include all of the folks who have had a impact on my life—friends, therapists, clients, family members, students, teachers, song writers, authors, pets.

But in the interest of conservation of our natural resources, I'll limit myself to the midwives who facilitated the pregnancy and are attending the birth.

Deepest appreciation to:

Kay King—for her artistic talent, patience, flexibility, sensitivity, trust

K.C. King—for her computer expertise, generosity, collaborative spirit

Marilyn Farwell—for her careful editing

My BAG group—for their love, intensity, constructive criticism, laughter

OR Innovative Publishers—for their experience and encouragement

My goddess network (you know who you are)

The tangueros

Order Form

To order more copies of *Ten Tips*, send to
T.C.C. Press
P.O. Box 50832
Eugene, OR 97405

Name_____

Address_____

City_____State_____Zip_____

Telephone_____

E-mail_____

Payment by check or money order only.
$10.95 per book plus $3.50 shipping cost for first
book and $.50 for each additional book

Order Form

To order more copies of *Ten Tips*, send to
T.C.C. Press
P.O. Box 50832
Eugene, OR 97405

Name_____

Address_____

City_____State_____Zip_____

Telephone_____

E-mail_____

Payment by check or money order only.
$10.95 per book plus $3.50 shipping cost for first
book and $.50 for each additional book